Mast

Learn the Power of Mind Control and Hypnotic Language Patterns (Basic to Advanced Conversational Hypnosis)

Noah-Jay Michael

Copyright

© 2014 by Noah-Jay Michael

ISBN: 978-1-312-28155-4

All rights reserved. No part of this book may be reproduced, copied, stored, or transmitted in any form or by any means, electronic, photographic, or mechanical, including photocopying, recording, or in any information storage and retrieval systems, without prior written permission of the author or publisher, except where permitted by law.

The information contained in this book is strictly for educational purposes. Therefore, if you wish to apply ideas contained in this book, you are taking full responsibility for your actions.

Disclaimer and Terms of Use

Any information provided in this book is through the author's interpretation. The author has done strenuous work to reassure the accuracy of this subject. If you wish you attempt any of the practices provided in this book, you are doing so with your own responsibility. The author will not be held accountable for any misinterpretations or misrepresentations of the information provided here.

All information provided is done so with every effort to represent the subject, but does not guarantee that your life will change. The author shall not be held liable for any direct or indirect damages that result from reading this book.

Contents

Copyright	2
Disclaimer and Terms of Use	3
1. Introduction	7
2. The Basics of Hypnosis	15
3. Conversational Hypnosis – The Basics	21
4. Some Basic Tools	27
5. Two Exercises for You	31
6. Why You Need Rapport	35
7. Rapport Tools – Mirroring and Matching	41
8. Rapport – What Can Go Wrong	47
9. Pulling In Your Audience	51
10. Hone Your Radar	57
11. Recognizing the Signals of Trance	61
12. Exercises for Rapport	65
13. What is Hypnotic Language?	69
14. Hypnotic Language Basics	73
15. Hypnotic Language Principles	77
16. Hypnotic Language Principles – Part 2	83
17. Hypnotic Language – The Agreement Pattern	89
18. Using the Agreement Pattern	95
19. Using Agreement Sets	99
20. Using Thought-Disruption Patterns	105
21. Using Conversational Hypnosis to Give Criticism	109

22.	The Importance of Confidence	115
23.	NLP Representational Systems	121
24.	Putting It All Together	127
25.	Conclusion	131

1. Introduction

Hypnosis is nothing new. In fact, it has been used for various reasons around the world since ancient times. The mysteries of the brain are still being explored but hypnosis and the principles upon which it is based are all based on how our brain processes information.

By knowing how the mind works, the conscious and the subconscious mind, it can be manipulated via hypnosis for entertainment or therapy purposes.

Conversational hypnosis is yet another form of hypnosis and it combines the same techniques as traditional hypnosis but in a more subtle fashion. Instead of putting someone into a deep trance, you are simply making it easier to influence and persuade them to listen to you.

You cannot force anyone to do anything against their will with hypnosis or conversational hypnosis but to those who do not understand how it works, it can be scary and that is how these myths are perpetuated.

Hypnosis is very misunderstood and because of that, it has somewhat of a bad reputation. This book is all about conversational hypnosis, or the art of persuasion. When you can speak and communicate to others in such a way that they not only listen and understand, but also respond to you in a positive manner, that is influence. Conversational hypnosis is nothing more than boosting the conversational skills you already have in order to be a better communicator.

There is no mystery or magic about it; these techniques have been in practice for hundreds of years. Any time you see someone who speaks easily and people just seem to gravitate to what they are saying, you can bet that they have mastered conversational hypnosis.

This book will not only make you a better speaker but it will also make you a more effective communicator.

What happens when you try to manipulate someone during a conversation? They get angry with you, right? If you try to force someone to agree to something they do not agree with or try to coerce them to do something they do not want to do, they will also become angry.

Once you try to use those negative tactics on someone, they will never respect you again. In fact, they will tell others that you tried to use shady tactics to get them to see things your way and your reputation will suffer.

Conversational Hypnosis is not manipulation. It is not forcing people to do anything against their will nor is it coercing them. Conversational hypnosis is simply a better way to communicate. It gives you command and control over the conversation in a positive way, so that there is no anger or ill will on the other person's part because there is no negative tactics such as manipulation.

Conversational hypnosis is learning how to communicate more effectively. When you communicate effectively, you are understood better and people will respond to you better.

Conversational hypnosis can be applied to every conversation you have, both in your personal life and professional life. In fact, for many, business professionals go out of their way to learn conversational hypnosis because it makes them more successful.

CEOs, owners, marketing professionals, salesmen, and more, who all rely on needing to communicate to people, often use conversational hypnosis to ensure that they are not only understood clearly but to help them become more persuasive.

Communication is how we go about your daily lives. Without it, conflicts arise and messages to each other become lost.

With conversational hypnosis, you will be able to gain an instant connection with the people you are speaking to, either individually or in a group. When you come across as someone who can be trusted, which instantly makes you credible and respected. People will find that speaking to you is a positive experience, and you will find that you can easily influence people through your communication.

That is the basis of conversation hypnosis, people can easily connect with you, understand what you are saying and they will connect with you easier because they can relate to you. Communication will never be the same; it will be better.

This book will explain how we communicate and relate to each other and will explain to you how to use that to your advantage. Conversational hypnosis is used by salespersons, speakers, CEOs, politicians and other influential speakers. The secrets to their great communication skills will now be yours.

There are five basic elements to conversation hypnosis.

- Relatable
- Understandable
- Confidence
- Executable
- Manageable

Relatable – If you can be relatable, the other person will respond to you better. When you speak, use a lot of anecdotes and examples to help others relate to what you are saying. This helps them relate what you are saying to their own lives and because it also gives them a link between you and the subject matter, they will connect better. If you are talking about something and you cannot relate to the subject, how can you expect others to?

Understandable – If they cannot understand what you are saying, they will not be able to respond the way you want. Using big words make you look smarter but when you fill your talk with unnecessary jargon and pretentious words, you lose people. They hear what you are saying but they do not understand it and that is the exact opposite of what you want. When you talk, the message needs to be understandable and clear for you to see results.

Confidence – Confidence is necessary because confidence is key to making conversational hypnosis work. You have to believe in what you say and you have to exude confidence and with that, you have to be accountable to yourself and to others in what you say you will do. For example, if you promise a favor to someone but you know you will not follow through, your demeanor will change because your confidence in your words will fail. You always speak the truth and your confidence will never falter.

Executable – Can you follow through with what you said? When what you say is executable, people will respect and admire you, and that gives you influence over them. The more people realize you mean what you say and that you execute it according to your own words, the more they will follow you.

Manageable – Is what you are saying managed well? Communication is partially what you say and partially how you say it. Can you manage both at the same time? You need to be able to use body language and verbal communication to manage your audience well.

Those are the basic elements of conversational hypnosis and in this book, we will explore the concepts and the techniques that make conversational hypnosis work and then the book will go into the advanced techniques, helping you hone the skills you are developing while adding new ones.

One of the focuses this book about advanced conversational hypnosis techniques has is all about hypnotic language. Humans process information in certain ways and our minds are geared toward responding to certain linguistic cues and language patterns.

When you combine these linguistic techniques, language patterns, and non-verbal communication, such as what you used to build rapport, you have a very powerful arsenal of language skills that will take your communication to a whole new level.

By taking advantage of these linguistic tricks, you can easily persuade people while having a simple conversation and they will not even know you are using any conversational hypnosis skills on them.

Hypnotic language is subtle but powerful and by the time you finish this book, you will be on your way to being a conversational hypnosis master.

2. The Basics of Hypnosis

Because conversational hypnosis includes the word hypnosis, people tend to confuse it with traditional hypnosis. When you are talking to someone, you are not covertly putting him or her under a hypnotic trance.

To more fully understand what conversational hypnosis is, you need to understand what hypnosis is and how it compares to conversational hypnosis.

Everyone knows what a hypnotist does, right? They do stage shows and they entertain, but there is a darker side perpetrated by the movies and media, of hypnotists hypnotizing people for their own nefarious plots. Keep in mind, movies are not real life.

Do hypnotists put people in a hypnotic trance for entertainment purposes? Yes, they do. However, they also help people with therapy as well.

Hypnotherapy has become an accepted and respectable practice but there is very little difference between how a stage hypnotist works and how a hypnotherapist works, aside from the end result. One is to entertain, the other to heal but the principles they use are the same. Those basics are also present to some degree with conversational hypnosis as well.

Conversational hypnosis is not conventional hypnosis. You are not going to ever have a person do anything that goes against their nature or against their will. Even regular hypnosis cannot make someone do anything that they would not normally do.

If asked to do something they are unwilling to do when under a hypnotic trance, they would simply come out of the trance. These are just some of the damaging myths that linger, giving hypnosis and conversational hypnosis a bad name.

What are the earmarks of hypnosis? Hypnosis has a specific goal. Hypnosis is achieved through the use of various tools. Hypnosis only works on people who want to be hypnotized and who allow it.

Hypnosis is only possible if the people fully trust and believe you. Those are the earmarks of any hypnosis session, no matter if it is for entertainment, hypnotherapy, or conversational hypnosis.

So, how can you use principles of hypnosis in a conversation? Easily, because hypnosis is all about influence, the only difference is the degree to which you have over them.

How do you influence people? By offering them an option that is mutually beneficial. Let me ask you a question. If you were to ask someone if they would like to help you with an unpleasant project or task, such as cutting down a big tree in your yard and you leave it open-ended, the odds are they will say no.

Why will they say no? They will say no because you gave them the opportunity to say no and there is nothing in it for them for offering to help you cut down a tree.

With conversational hypnosis, you will learn how to approach that type of situation so you can present your audience with a win-win situation so that they are not presented with a yes or no question, but a yes-yes question where they are going to want to say yes because it will benefit them as well.

Learning how to phrase things is part of conversational hypnosis and that will help you be able to influence. How does this connect with the earmarks of hypnosis listed above?

When you are talking to someone, you have a specific goal; there is either something that you want them to do or agree to. You use language and body language tools to help achieve your conversational hypnosis goals.

Conversational hypnosis is only possible when your audience trusts and believes in you. You will not be able to make anyone to do something they do not want to.

That covers all of the earmarks of hypnosis. Even though it is different from stage hypnosis or hypnotherapy, conversational hypnosis is still a type of hypnosis so the earmarks, or basics, all apply.

What is hypnosis really? The short answer is that hypnosis is a mindset that is altered, or an altered way of thinking. Normally, our active thinking dictates what we are saying and doing and hypnosis is a shortcut to the subconscious mind. The type of hypnosis dictates the degree in which the subconscious is accessed. However, the same rules and earmarks as discussed above still apply.

When you are speaking directly to someone's subconscious, you have effectively bypassed the guard, the active thinking. This is why you can easily influence people when they are hypnotized. Once again, I want to reinforce that you will not be able to influence anyone to do anything they are not willing to do. That is just a myth.

With conversational hypnosis, you are using hypnosis techniques that make your communication more effective because the person or people you are speaking to will easily key into the parts of your speech that you want them to. There are those who say that is not effective or that you are placing undue influence on a person by "messing with their mind".

Keep in mind, hypnosis is actually a naturally occurring event. We hypnotize ourselves all the time. Have you ever zoned out when driving, walking, running, or when doing any other repetitive task?

Chances are that you will say yes. When you do that, you have actually entered into a light hypnotic trance. You are still in full control of your actions, right? Of course you are! That is how hypnosis works. Using the same principles that put people in a trance, including yourself, you can actually use hypnosis to impress the importance of what you are saying to another person.

You are not taking away their free will. You are just using tools that encourage people to become engrossed in what you are saying.

Have you ever heard someone talk who was just so charismatic that you could not stop listening, even though you might not have originally been interested in what they had to say? If so, that is conversational hypnosis at work. Those are the tools you will learn, to be a great speaker and an effective communicator.

Our brains are hard wired to respond to certain things in a certain manner. Hypnosis knows all about these responses and the tools the hypnotist uses all centers around how to trigger certain responses.

We know how and why people will respond to certain stimuli so we actively use that stimuli to trigger a response we want. That is how conversational hypnosis works. For this to work, you need to learn to read people.

How often do you pay attention to the verbal and physical clues that the person you are talking to is giving off? You probably have not paid very much attention. However, if you start paying attention, you can tell when they are beginning to become annoyed, agitated, friendly, or relaxed and you can tailor your responses around their responses. You will learn how to tell what the other person that you are talking to is reacting to you and to use that to your advantage.

Speaking should be effective. Communication should be clear and reactionary. Conversational hypnosis allows you to react and keep the communication on a positive note.

Imagine, no more arguments that get you nowhere and instead, having conversations that results! That is the power of conversational hypnosis and that power is about to be yours.

3. Conversational Hypnosis – The Basics

Now that you have a better understanding of hypnosis, it is time to get into the basics of conversational hypnosis.

Knowing that hypnosis is a natural state of mind, you will be able to use tools to help people enter that slight trance state, making them suggestive so that they will be more apt to respond to you. You are not forcing or coercing them in any way and if it is something they are against doing, they will not do it. The light hypnotic trance will be broken and you will need to rebuild that connection.

That is how hypnosis works; if you try to force something, the trance simply breaks because it is one of the brain's safety measures.

What conversational hypnosis does do is allow you to converse easily, in harmony. Even debates with varying opinions are made without heated arguments. If talking to others is a big part of your life, especially for work, then conversational hypnosis will help you.

Just like any other tool, it is a way for you to help facilitate the impact your conversations have with people.

There are a few steps to making conversational hypnosis work well. The first part is that you have to draw their attention to what you want them to focus on.

Charismatic speakers are great at drawing your attention in, and it is not only because they pepper their talk with jokes or funny anecdotes but also because they know how to draw your attention to what they are saying. They speak so clearly, you can practically envision what they are talking about in your mind.

That is your goal with conversational hypnosis; you need to be able draw the people you are talking to what you are saying.

It was mentioned earlier that hypnosis is a shortcut to the subconscious, bypassing the conscious mind. Our conscious mind is our critical thinking center, it is where we reason and filter things out that we deem unnecessary or detrimental to our subconscious.

For example, whenever you see a salesperson, your first thought would be, "I do not want to be roped into listening to a sales pitch for whatever they are selling because I do not need that product." Your conscious mind tells you that listening to the sales pitch is a bad idea because it has already determined that you do not need to buy whatever it is they are selling and so your guard goes up and you are wary and skeptical.

Conversational hypnosis helps you lower or drop that guard in other people, so you can speak to them without the conscious thinking being too critical about things. People are naturally skeptical, that is how they protect themselves.

You will learn how to sidestep the part of their mind that does the critical thinking because that is where the resistance comes from. Sidestep the critical thinking area and you can easily influence people.

This is what is meant by being in harmony; that is, when you and someone else are talking and feel connected. When you are in harmony, your audience is less resistant to your train of thought and you are more likely to be able to speak to them and influence them without triggering their skeptical critical thinking area.

Let us go back to the salesperson example. How many times have you thought that you would not buy a product but you stayed for the sales pitch and then you ended up buying the product?

You had every intention of not buying it but now you own one. That is because the salesperson used conversational hypnosis to sneak past your critical thinking center and without your skeptical defenses up and ready, you ended up buying the product. You were drawn in, you listened, you agreed, and you made the purchase, all of your own free will; that is the power you will have.

How does conversational hypnosis work? You use triggers designed to elicit responses from your audience's subconscious mind. When push comes to shove, the subconscious mind has most of the power because it is the biggest part of your thinking process; that is why the conscious mind protects it so fiercely.

Humans are emotional creatures and the heart of our emotions is firmly ingrained in our subconscious thinking.

If you can trigger an emotional response in someone, then you can influence him or her. Once you can trigger that emotional response, you are able to help influence their decision making, in your favor. Trust, believability, and other factors all help make you credible to your audience so when you can talk and it triggers an emotion, which helps them to connect to you.

Why is it so important to make them to respond to you an emotional level? It is important because emotions are so tied into the subconscious, that once you trigger an emotional response, you will have established rapport and that is how you can begin to influence.

You are always in control of the conversation when you are using conversational hypnosis; the minute you lose control of the conversation, you lose your ability to influence.

With conversational hypnosis, you gently steer your audience into making the responses you want them to make. Instead of allowing them a yes or no response, you gently lead them to saying yes by not allowing no to be a choice. You will learn all of these later in the book.

Conversational hypnosis is very subtle. The people you are talking to will not even know that they are being influenced. To them, you are just very charismatic, charming, and a great speaker; they will have no idea you are using conversational hypnosis during your conversation. It has to be subtle to be effective.

You cannot make anybody say yes to you, but you can lead him or her into saying yes because there is a benefit to saying it. You can help them see why yes is the right answer to make instead of no.

Conversational hypnosis is like the tides, it requires an ebb and flow of the conversation, flowing between you and your audience. If they are not participating, then it is harder to engage them.

4. Some Basic Tools

There are many tools you will use with conversational hypnosis. It is not just any one tool that makes this effective, but rather, the combination of all of them.

In this section, you will become familiar with some of the basic tools conversational hypnosis uses. This will be a brief overview of some of your basic tools and how to use them that will help you with conversational hypnosis.

Yes Mindset

Do you know why it is so hard to make someone to change their mind? Because once they have made up their minds to say no, it is hard to make them to switch that no to a yes. A yes mindset is how you turn those no's into yes's and it is easier than you might think.

It is easy to say no to something, as long as you stand firm and just say no. However, once you say yes to something, even something seemingly unrelated, it becomes harder to maintain your position on saying no.

Once someone starts to say yes, it is easier to make them begin agreeing with you. You just need to have them to say that first yes and that helps them move into the yes mindset.

Once you have them in a positive frame of mind, then it is easier to steer them into saying yes. You are not coercing, just leading.

For example, if you are selling a laptop, you ask someone if they like a laptop that is user friendly. Most people will say yes, because you are not selling them that laptop, not yet; you are just putting them in the yes mindset. Once they begin to say yes, it will be easier to influence them into saying yes about buying that laptop.

As you can see, the way to set up the yes mindset is rather indirect and that is because the conscious does not catch that there is anything wrong with saying yes to such an innocent question.

Once they say yes to that, you can ask if they like a laptop that has a long battery life, something else they will say yes to. You can go on like that, having them indirectly agreeing to the best features of the laptops so by the time you actually give them the sales pitch, they will be so used to saying yes to you, it will be their first instinct to say yes to the laptop rather than no.

Setting up the yes mindset early on is best, so start off with a question they simply should not be able to say no to. It does not have to be related to the topic, just something that they can answer yes to, and preferably, something positive. The yes mindset questions should not be things they have to think about, they should be easy to answer so that the yes just rolls off the tip of their tongue without them having to think about it.

Once they start to think about it, they will begin to analyze it and then their conscious thinking will become skeptical and will be on guard. If it is a nice day out, even something as basic as, "It sure is a sunny day outside, is it not?" is a good way to put them in the yes mindset.

Embedded Commands

Embedded commands allow you to suggest things without really suggesting them. You imply something or suggest it, instead of coming out and just saying it and that makes it a very effective tool for influence. Embedded commands are the fastest way to get into the subconscious mind.

Embedded commands are subtle, so the conscious mind does not filter them out, and so the subconscious mind picks up on the embedded commands, giving them more weight and thus, allowing you to use these embedded commands to influence.

Remember how the subconscious is where the decisions are really made? If you influence the subconscious, you influence the decision and that is how embedded commands work.

If you want to subtly start to get someone thinking about buying a faster laptop, such as what you are selling, you can tell them "How do you feel when your laptop is slow to boot up?" The words you and feel are trigger words for an emotional response. Naturally, everyone is frustrated with a slow laptop and you have the solution!

When you are using embedded commands, you use words that you emphasis just slightly, words that will elicit a response, a positive response from your audience. You will be amazed at how much power certain words have behind them when you emphasis them slightly. The subconscious picks up on that slight emphasis and tells that person to pay attention to those words.

Minimizing resistance is the entire goal of conversational hypnosis and all of the tools you will use are designed to minimize resistance to what you are suggesting. This involves you engaging your audience verbally, getting a feel for what they want so you can give it to them. There is no script with conversation hypnosis because how one person reacts will not be the same as how another person reacts.

You need to be quick on your feet and be able to smoothly react and redirect the conversation as needed. Naturally, because it is all so subtle, it will take a lot of practice on your part but practicing is easy. It takes a while to be comfortable enough with all conversational hypnosis to be able to go out and fluidly use it well but you will be able to. Just like anything, persistence and patience is the key.

5. Two Exercises for You

Reading about it is one thing, but practicing is another so this chapter will have a few quick exercises for you so you become accustomed to some of the basics of hypnosis.

Being able to pay attention to someone's body language, tone, and words are all necessary and to be a great communicator, you have to constantly monitor all three aspects of communication, which are nonverbal, verbal, and vocal communication.

Vocal communication is about how they say it, not what they say. Verbal is about what they say and nonverbal is their body language and facial expressions. If you are not a people watcher, become one. You need to ramp up your radar and start paying attention to people.

The first exercise is to be able to pay enough attention to be able to tell when people are in a natural hypnotic state.

In an earlier chapter, natural hypnosis was mentioned, now you must put your skills to the test to find people who are "in the zone" and in a hypnotic state. How can you tell? Look for people who are hyper-focused on what they are doing, so wrapped up in their actions and their thoughts that they are not paying attention to anything else around them.

This will help you be able to get non-verbal cues from people so when you are ready to start using conversational hypnosis, you can easily tell who is in the zone and suggestible and who is still going to be resistant. Go out somewhere, a park, a library or a coffee shop even and just sit and watch the other people. Find someone who is focused and not paying any attention to anything on around them.

Take note of how his actions and demeanor is different from someone who is not focused on anything on particular. What sets that person apart from the people around them, the ones who are not "in the zone"?

Look for cues in their body language and in their speech, if they are interacting verbally with someone. Do this with several people so you are easily able to spot someone "in the zone" and know what to look for.

The second part of the exercise is you need to start being comfortable talking to people and you need to be able to grab and to hold their attention. Therefore, this is a chance for you to show off your people skills.

In short, how effective are you at getting people to pay attention to you. Now, you can use bizarre methods to encourage people to pay attention to you, but will that make them continue paying attention to you? This is a two-part exercise, get their attention and then hold it.

You can do this anywhere but populated places are best. Choose a place where there are many people to talk to, such as a park, café, coffee shop, etc. If you have trouble talking to strangers, this is perfect for you because you have to get over any lingering shyness about talking to people.

With conversational hypnosis, you have to be confident, cool, and collected, not nervous and jittery; so if you are afraid of talking to people, you have to get over that and this exercise will help you with this. You need to be 100% comfortable with talking to people for you to use conversational hypnosis.

Start talking to people; see how long you can hold a stranger's attention without forcing the issue. You need to make them want to keep talking to you so turn up your charisma and start talking.

This is an exercise that leads into our next chapter, how to establish rapport. For right now, you just need to see if you can make someone to begin talking to you and for how long. You can use jokes, you can use small talk, or you can dazzle them with trivia; it does not matter how, only that you can grab and hold their attention.

If this makes you uncomfortable, practice it until you are fully comfortable. You are sharpening your social skills and your comfort factor with talking to people. There is no real goal other than to try to hold their attention for longer and longer with each new person you talk to. Expect some people to just brush off your attempts to talk to them, which is normal; just go onto the next person.

You cannot be discouraged because rejection is part of life. If someone is resistant to talking to you, just let them go and shrug it off. Conversation should be flowing so you can keep their interest. This is important because in the next chapter, we will go over the importance of rapport, and that will require you to be comfortable talking to people, to find common ground.

People love to talk about things they have in common so try to find some common ground with the strangers you are talking to, to help facilitate the conversation and keep it going. Start off slow with this one, help yourself shake off any doubts or fear about approaching strangers for a conversation.

This beginning exercise helps you shed any self-doubts and to build up your confidence about speaking to people.

6. Why You Need Rapport

Have you ever sat down next to a stranger, started a conversation, and then just hit it off with them so the conversation fell into an easy flow? If so, that is an example of rapport.

Rapport is an invisible connection between you and someone else that helps them trust you and connect with you. Rapport is important because without rapport, hypnosis will not work. Rapport is the foundation for being able to hypnotize someone or for conversational hypnosis to work.

Why is rapport so important? Would you believe someone you had no connection with or you had no reason to trust? Probably not because if your conscious is throwing up warning signs, you will not let your guard down enough for that person to be able to influence you.

However, if someone feels comfortable with you and feels like you are trusted, then they will relax their guard and you will be able to influence them better.

An early chapter mentioned harmony and when you are in harmony with someone, you have established rapport. Rapport helps communication go better, clearer, and with less distrust and miscommunication. Rapport is that easy feeling of being comfortable with someone and once you learn to establish rapport with people, you will be on your way to being able to use conversational hypnosis.

You already know how to establish rapport. When you get together with your friends and family, you establish it instantly. However, let us say that the one cousin you never get along with comes to the party, you will have trouble establishing rapport because they are someone who you either dislike or disagree with.

You can establish rapport with nearly anyone and the most charismatic people can instantly establish rapport.

We all use rapport to help get what we want. Children, when caught doing something they should not will counter their parent's anger with a compliment because they know that if they tell their mom that they love her dress, she will be less mad about the crayon on the walls. If you want to butter up a co-worker to help you with a project, you will first compliment them on their last project.

Rapport is an ingrained social skill we all learn and now you will just be able to better leverage it as a conversation tool to influence.

To establish rapport, you have to carefully clue into someone's verbal and non-verbal clues. There are various ways to establish rapport and you just need to keep using them until you find the one that works best with the person you are talking to.

If you do not feel like you are establishing rapport with one method, smoothly move onto the next one.

Now, how and why does rapport work so well? The reason rapport works is tied into human nature. Humans are programed to be suspicious of things that are not like them and to trust things that are similar. This is an old instinct that helped our ancestors stay alive and it has not gone away.

In short, we like things that are familiar because they make us comfortable. People are more comfortable with things that are familiar to them than with things they are not familiar with. Birds of a feather flock together; even that old adage tips its hat to this basic part of human nature.

We like things that remind us of ourselves. Why? Well, we know we are trustworthy so if something reminds us of ourselves, we tend to trust that thing or that person because they are familiar.

With conversational hypnosis, you need to learn how to establish rapport so people will have that instant connection to you, so they feel familiar with you and trust you better.

Which salesperson are you most likely to buy from? One who stands behind the counter and mechanically recites their sales pitch without making any attempt to personalize the experience or make eye contact, or the salesperson who makes eye contact, speaks naturally and with emotion, and uses personal anecdotes and examples in a sales pitch that were more informative than sales pitch?

You would buy from the second salesperson, right? Naturally, because they established rapport and built a connection with you and that made you feel comfortable so you trusted what they said more.

The thing is, the first person had the better product but the second salesperson had the better rapport and sales pitch so you ended up with the less durable product instead of the better product.

Rapport is so important, sales managers often will send sales trainees to seminars and workshops to learn how to establish rapport and to master conversational hypnosis. These are proven techniques and the foundation of it all is rapport.

How do you make yourself familiar to the person you are talking to? Well, you can use verbal ways. The salesperson in the example used examples and anecdotes to connect you to them.

When you outline similarities, or even indirectly mention them, it helps to establish rapport. Once the seed has been planted that you and they have something in common, rapport is easy to establish.

The more you can make them see the similarities between you and them, the more they will drop their guard. Have you ever noticed that salespersons always find something in common to talk about with you?

That is not by accident, they are establishing rapport. Start talking and find some common ground. Once you do find it, make sure to subtly highlight that you have something in common. Common bonds not only give you something to talk about, but it is also that first step toward establishing rapport.

The more you establish that you are familiar, the more unguarded they become. They relax, they start to believe you and trust you, and that makes it easier for you to be able to influence them later on. Remember, you are not trying to force or coerce them, just influence them, so you are not going to hit them up with your requests right away.

Just take time to chat, to establish that common ground. This is necessary because without common ground, no matter how much chitchat you engage in, you will lack rapport.

You want to be seen as a friend, someone who is on their side. If you are their friend, you would not steer them wrong, at least, that is what their subconscious will be telling them. Familiar equals trusted so if you want to be trusted, you have to be familiar. This is why you take the time to be friendly, to ask about them to find that common ground and establish rapport.

7. Rapport Tools – Mirroring and Matching

Mirroring and matching are two tools used for establishing rapport. As stated in the prior chapter, people feel more comfortable around people who are familiar to them.

When we see something that is familiar to us, our subconscious tells us we can trust the person who is similar to us because they are familiar. The problem is, how do you meet someone and then make them feel as if you are familiar and trusted, so you can quickly establish rapport?

The best way to make someone feel as if you are familiar to them is to make yourself as similar to them as you can. Mirroring and matching are two subtle ways you can adapt your mannerisms and body language to be similar to the person you are talking to. This is a subtle way that makes you seem similar to them and so they will relax their guard, feeling as if you are trusted.

Does this mean you do whatever they do? No, this is not a game of monkey see monkey do like you played in school or as a kid. Mirroring and matching, when done right, is very subtle but extremely effective. Here is an example to illustrate.

Who would you rather have a discussion with, someone who speaks much faster than you or someone who speaks with a similar rate of speech to your own? You would rather speak to the person who has a similar rate of speech of yourself, naturally. Why?

Because it is familiar to you, it reminds you of yourself and so you trust the person who speaks like you do more than the person who speaks radically different from you.

Mirroring and matching are easy to learn and help to create rapport almost instantly. If you are ever in a conversation and you feel like you are losing your audience or in danger of losing your connection, use mirroring and matching to bolster your connection so you do not lose your rapport with your audience.

Once you get the hang of these tools, they will be your go-to tools for whenever you want someone to feel at ease when you are talking to them.

What exactly is mirroring and matching? Simply put, you copy (mirroring and matching) someone else's verbal and speech style and pattern and their body language.

It creates a common factor between the two of you that the other person may not actively notice but their subconscious will. Once their subconscious realizes that you sound similar and your body language is familiar, it will decide you are familiar, and therefore, trustworthy.

You mirror and match subtly, so it is not obvious. That is the only tricky part about this, learning to be subtle about matching their mannerisms and vocal style. If you are caught copying the other person, not only will you not be able to establish rapport, but you will also lose their trust, which is why you need to be subtle. You want to subtly copy them but not look like you are mocking them through mimicry.

You need to pay attention to their basic body language, including how they are sitting or standing and some of the motions they make such as straightening a tie or tucking hair behind their ear.

If they are sitting leaning forward, you should sit leaning forward as well. If they have a very unusual stance or habit, then do not try to copy that because it would be too obvious. You do not have to match it exactly, just come close to it.

If they shift position, do not rush to switch your position right away; wait a little bit and then casual shift to a new position that is similar to their own. You can easily help someone feel at ease by matching body language. This is the same for actions other people take as well.

Now, because you are not always speaking to people of the same gender, you can use a comparable motion to mirror and match what they have just done.

I am talking about the mindless types of actions people tend to do when talking, common actions or nervous actions they tend to do a lot. For example, if you are a male speaking to a female and she has a tendency to smooth down the front of her shirt when she is talking then you can straighten your tie every now and then. It is not an exact copy but it is similar enough to trigger that connection.

If someone with long hair tucks their hair behind their ear when they are talking and you have short hair, just run your hand over your hair as if to smooth it in place. Comparable actions work equally well. It is amazing how such a simple thing can help establish trust but it can and it will. It works almost instantly.

When talking to someone, just observe them to see if they have any repeated mannerisms and then you can start using, in moderation, the same or comparable mannerisms yourself, while continuing to mirror and match their body language. The idea is to, every now and then, use one of their mannerisms, without going overboard.

Even their breathing can be mirrored and matched; note when they inhale, exhale, and change your breathing so you are breathing in time with them. This is another very subtle tool but surprisingly effective and incredibly easy to do. This is the first thing you should do when meeting someone and it is nearly impossible to be caught doing this.

In addition to their body language, you need to match their verbal style. Let me be clear. You are not to suddenly adopt an accent if you do not have one and do not mimic a speech impediment.

What you should do is to mirror and match their rate of speech, their speech volume, and if they have any phrases or words they use a lot, to use a few of those same words or phrases, every now and then when you talking.

Once someone starts to talk, you can quickly measure how fast or how slow they talk. You should adjust your rate of speech so you are talking at the same rate of speech. So if they are a fast talker, you need to talk fast as well and if they are a slow talker, you will need to slow down your rate of speech.

Same with volume, if you are talking to someone who has a very soft voice and you are naturally loud, it can be really off-putting to them and it will make them apprehensive about trusting you. We feel comfortable with things that are familiar so you make yourself familiar to them, that is how mirroring and matching works.

8. Rapport – What Can Go Wrong

Although establishing rapport can be easy, a lot can go wrong. This chapter is about what can go wrong and why you might be having trouble establishing rapport. By learning what some of the common mistakes are, you can be aware of them and take care to avoid making these very same mistakes.

Too Many Compliments

It is natural to want to compliment your audience, to encourage them to like you and to be more receptive to listening to you. However, when you slather on the compliments thickly, they quickly sound fake and like a ploy to make them like you.

Once you do anything to arouse suspicion, you will find establishing rapport will be almost impossible. You need to be nice to the person you are talking to but you can be too nice and that comes across as fake.

You want to be believable and that means you need to avoid all appearances of being fake, which is why you cannot be too heavy handed on the compliments.

Once you start using too many compliments, or saying things that are very obviously not true, you transition from a likeable and respected person of authority and right into a shady used car dealer with a fake smile trying to sell a lemon.

Communication is ultimately about the other person receiving and understanding the message you want them to get. When you focus on being too nice, your message becomes lost and that allows the message to become lost. Your focus is on getting your message through, politely and clearly.

Trying Too Hard

Conversational hypnosis is not about coercion and sometimes, you have to realize you will not get what you want. When that happens, you need to walk away.

If you are trying to sell your point too forcibly, you will end up making the other person put up their guard because they will suspect that there is something you want from them. You need to stay even and pleasant and avoid any hint of pressure or desperation in your talk.

Once you come across as desperate, the other person's warning bells will go off and you will lose the connection. Desperate is bad, so avoid trying so hard to get your point across that you come off as desperate.

Would you buy a product from a salesperson who was practically begging people to buy? No, of course not! You would become suspicious and pass on the product and the same principle holds true here, your desperation will make them suspicious of whatever you are selling or suggesting and they will have already made up their mind to say no.

Not Being Genuine

Remember the example of the salesperson who was just mechanically reading their sales speech and the salesperson who was enthusiastic about the product, talking about how much they love it and why?

You need to be the second person because if you are not genuinely interested or excited about what you have to say, neither will anyone else. If you are not showing genuine interest, your audience will never be able to connect with you or your message.

What happens if you are having a bad day and you have to go into a big sales pitch meeting? You put that bad day behind you and you go in there with enthusiasm, energy, and passion.

You have to be passionate about what you are talking about or selling. You want to engage and interact and people connect easier to someone who is showing emotion, and enthusiasm is contagious!

Even if you have given your speech a hundred times, you give it with as much enthusiasm for the hundred and first time as you did the first time. Your voice, your face, and your body language needs to say you care and you are passionate.

Your lack of emotion, interest, and passion can keep you from establishing rapport.

Mirroring and Matching Errors

We mentioned a few of the mistakes in the prior chapter that you can make with mirroring and matching. If you instantly copy every single action the person you are talking to makes, you will be caught and they will think you are mocking them. Do not rush to copy movements, do them slowly and naturally, and wait a while to even begin to match your body language to theirs.

Never try to mirror or match facial tics or any sort of tic or involuntary motion, which will just come off as if you are making fun of them.

Similarly, if they have a lisp, do not try to mirror and match that or any speech impediment. If they have an accent, it can be tempting to automatically fall into that same accent, and it is easy to do it without realizing you are doing it but you have to pay attention to make sure that you aren't doing that.

The above are the main errors that will either break rapport or make it hard to establish in the first place. Make sure you take care to avoid any of the above when you are speaking to people and you will find that you can make and keep rapport established easier.

9. Pulling In Your Audience

It is important that you not only grab your audience's attention but that you also create an interest for them to keep listening.

You want to create a bond, and that is what rapport is for, but once you establish rapport, you need to keep pulling in your audience so they are hooked. It is kind of clichéd but it is a good analogy so you can compare conversational hypnosis to fishing. You get the fish to pay attention to your bait but if you reel in too early, you miss the fish.

You have to do the same thing with your audience. If you reel in too early, then you lose them. You have to tantalize them with your bait, which is the early part of your speech, the part that hooks them and holds their interest before you reel them in. You can use various methods to help hook their attention, pulling them deeper into rapport.

One such tool to hook them in is to tell part of a story, but not the whole story. You never play your full hand right up front so you tell them just enough to get them interested so they want to keep listening to you.

Tell stories and give anecdotes that tell most of, but not all of, an interesting story. Leave them wanting more, so they engage you in banter and conversation. Once you have them engaged in conversation, you can easily keep pulling them in.

You should do this the entire time you are talking because it ensures your audience does not lose interest. What you are doing is helping to build up expectation because they will expect you to fill in the missing information at some point; and you will, just not all at once. This is a valuable tool to help grab and keep interest.

The goal is to make the person you are talking ask you questions, to get that back and forth flow of the conversation going and to keep it going. An example of this would be along the lines of "This reminds me of the time I was attending a conference. It was several states away, so I flew. Well, my friend, Murphy's Law, decided to show up and to say that it was an interest day is an understatement! To make a long story short, I did make the conference, barely."

The audience knows that something happened, but not what. If they want to know the details, they have to ask you and chances are, they will! That is how you can leave out information to pull in your audience because you are engaging our natural curiosity. When they are curious, they begin to ask questions.

Why is it so important to get them to start asking questions?

For one, if they are asking questions, that means you are not trying to rush or pressure them for whatever you want because you are taking the time to answer their questions and in fact, you are encouraging them. You are giving them time and space to think about what you are saying, and ask you about it.

When a salesperson is trying to rush you into a decision, you become wary, right? Anyone would. When they see you are not pressuring them, and engaging them in an actual conversation instead of just giving them a sales pitch, they will immediately trust you more.

Once you have their trust, you can easily influence them. Influence is only possible with trust and that is why all of the conversational hypnosis tools in this book involve making people feel comfortable and getting them to trust you.

Trust is how you help hold that connection with someone. You would not be taking the time to answer questions if you had something to hide or a hidden agenda, so they start to trust you more simply because you are taking time to speak to them. They will not even notice that you are engineering the conversation to encourage them to ask the questions in the first place.

Here is another example of how to leave out information to help grab their attention and pull them in, helping to engage them in conversation.

In this example, I will show you how to link your goal with your hook statement. Let us say that you are selling a health supplement that helps boost the immune system. You can say, "There is a village in South America, near the rainforest and the people who live there rarely sick. Colds, the flu, and other common illnesses occur less frequently there than in the surrounding cities. Wouldn't it be great if you could be sick less, too?"

In our example, when questioned, the speaker will go onto explain that a common plant in the area, which is used in their cooking, is actually the reason their immune system is so strong and that same plant is in your health supplements.

Can you see how you can use these conversational hypnosis hooks to grab your audience's attention and pull it in, making them want more, and ultimately, leading them into doing what you are guiding them into doing? It is a simple, yet effective conversational tool.

==As humans, our curiosity is piqued when we know we have part of the information but not all of it.== In the above example, the speaker left out the name of the city and the cause of the village's increased resistance to common illnesses. People listening will be naturally curious about this and will want to know more.

Who does not want to be healthier? If it works for that village, it must work for others. You are carefully generating interest that helps lead them to your goal. This low-pressure approach will always work better than a hard sell approach, every single time.

10. Hone Your Radar

You need to have your radar on and alert when you are using conversational hypnosis because you have to be able to quickly see the signals and clues your audience is putting off so you can change your tactics, if need be, to make what you are saying more effective. If you ignore the signals the person you are talking to is giving off, you are ignoring the chance to help fortify your connection with them if it is weakening.

Here is an example that has two salespersons, both selling televisions. One sees a customer come over and begins to explain the features on the largest TV. The customer glances at the price tag and shakes their head slightly but the salesperson continues trying to extol the benefits and features of that TV. In the end, the customer leaves the store.

The second customer comes and looks at the same TV but the second salesperson comes over to help them. When highlighting some of the TV's best features, the salesperson sees that the customer looks at the price tag and makes a face and instead of continuing to talk about that TV, he shows the customer another TV, with the same features, but a lower price and he gets the sale.

By ignoring the first customer's body language, the first salesperson lost the sale. You have to be an active listener as well as keep your body language radar on and on high. You are looking for verbal and physical clues that they are either agreeing or disagreeing with you when you are talking. Once you hone your radar and see the clues they are giving you about what they are thinking or feeling as a reaction to what you are saying, you can easily adjust your sails, so to speak, to steer the conversation back in the direction you want.

Excellent communicators always seem to be able to anticipate the needs of their audience. They are not psychic, they are just using their signal radar to read their audience and respond instantly to the clues and signs they are seeing. That is what you need to do.

It is so easy to just zone out when you are talking and not pay attention to whom you are talking to but you cannot do that. You have to be listening for verbal cues and watching for visual ones the entire time you are talking.

People give off signals all the time. You know most of them, you just tend to not relate them to what you are saying when you see them but you need to start paying attention and to relate them to your talk. Their tone, words, and body language all need to be constantly monitored because those are what your radar is going to be focused on.

You can use these signals to help bridge your connection to your audience as well. It is amazing what you can learn when you start being observant.

For example, if you see someone glance at their watch, that is a sign that they are either bored or in a hurry. Seeing someone standing or sitting with closed off posture, such as with their arms crossed over their chest, is usually a sign that you have not established rapport and they are closed off to what you have to say.

If they are nodding along with what you are saying, they are paying attention. Those are examples of some of the little signals you need to start paying attention to.

Here is an exercise for learning to read body language:

Actors not only have to read lines, but they have to act the part and that means their body language has to match what they are saying and it has to convey their feelings as well. When you watch someone act, you are not just listening to them but you are watching them convey emotion and feeling through their facial expressions and their body language.

Actors, at least the best ones, are masters of body language signals because if their body language did not match, they would not be very good actors. Pick a DVD, preferably one you have not memorized, because you are about to test your body language skills. Put the DVD in and start the movie but mute the sound. That is right, keep the sound muted and try to figure out what is happening by watching their faces and their body language. Make sure that you do not have the subtitles on either.

You need to rely only on what you see, not what you read or hear.

Take notes for the first fifteen minutes of the movie. What do you think the characters are thinking or feeling? Pause and rewind if you need to, but go about fifteen minutes into the movie, taking notes about what you think is going on. Now, go back to the beginning and turn the sound back on. Watch it with the sound and see how close you were to being right.

When you reach where you had stopped, after fifteen minutes, mute it once again and watch another fifteen minutes, trying to decide what they are doing without the benefit of sound. After you have taken notes, then you can go back and watch it with sound. Do this for the entire movie.

By the time you watch several movies in this manner, you will have honed your body language radar to the point where you can easily read body language. If you are still having trouble reading the body language without the sound, keep watching movies in this manner until you start getting the body language right more often than you get it wrong.

Once you have this exercise down, you can start going out to a park or a café and just watch the body language of the people around you. See if you can tell what they are feeling or thinking based on their body language. You should be an expert by this time.

11. Recognizing the Signals of Trance

During clinical or stage hypnosis, trance is something that is induced by the hypnotist. In conversational hypnosis, you are still inducing a hypnotic trance and there are varying degrees of hypnotic trance.

Naturally, a stage hypnotist will want to have a deep trance induced but for conversational hypnosis, that is not necessary. You start to put them in a trance when you begin to build rapport and then you work to deepen the trance as you talk to them.

Below are the signals of being in trance, so you can easily tell where your audience is when you are talking to them.

Signal One

When we are consciously thinking, our pupils are contracted (unless they are in a dim room). The first thing that will tell you is that your audience is beginning to enter trance. Once you have established rapport, the other person will begin to relax and his subconscious will be unguarded, and that is when the pupils will begin to dilate.

[Handwritten note: Pupils also dilate when looking at someone/thing enjoyable. Do not let this be your only sign.]

When you see dilated pupils, you know that you more than have their attention, you have them interested and they are listening to you without the wariness most people have when speaking to someone they do not know. It shows that rapport is there and that they are comfortable with you.

Signal Two

In addition to seeing dilated pupils, someone's pulse rate will slow down when you are talking to them. Hypnotists will sometimes hold onto their subject's hand or wrist when inducing them because they can monitor their pulse. This is not practical for conversational hypnosis, naturally, but if their neck is visible, you can usually see the pulse in the vein in their neck.

Not everyone can have their pulse monitored in this way because their neck may be thick, or their vein may not be as close to the surface as some people's veins are. But, if you can see their pulse in their neck, even just slightly, make note of how quickly their pulse is going when you first start talking and then again when you see their pupils dilate. You will see that as they become comfortable and relaxed, their pulse will slow. If you see it become more pronounced at any time after slowing, that means they are becoming agitated.

Reversely, if you are trying to pump up your audience, you want to see their pulse jump. Therefore, you can use it to gauge their emotional state and then change your words to the result you want, to continue either to relax them or to energize them.

Signal Three

Always take note of your audience's rate of breathing and the way they are breathing. You should take note of this anyway because you should be mirroring and matching their breathing to establish rapport. However, you need to take note because as they go into trance, they will alter their breathing and you need to be able to notice this change in the breathing.

Just like the pulse, if you are trying to pump up your audience, their breathing rate will increase but if you are trying to relax them, to encourage them to trust you and to enter that quieter type of trance, then their breathing will slow down.

Signal Four

You can tell from looking at someone's face what his or her state of mind is. You can take a quick glance at their face to tell you if what you are saying is having the desired effect. Someone who is entering trance and is relaxing will have a relaxed face. You will see that their features have smoothed out, so no wrinkled forehead or pursed lips; the face will be somewhat slack because they will be relaxed.

Signal Five

If they are not interested, they will not be paying close attention to you. If you see them studying the people around them, glancing at something in their hand, or just unfocused in general, you do not have their attention. If they are in trance and listening to you, they will be paying extra attention to you. This is how you know you have them hooked.

Are they focused on you? If their eyes are toward you but slightly unfocused, they are probably paying close attention to what you are saying, which is why they are using their hearing more than their vision at that point; they have their eyes on autopilot when they listen to you closely.

Signal Six

If you see them begin to make subconscious responses to what you are saying, that means they are in trance and in harmony with you. Conscious responses are deliberate actions they chose to make and subconscious responses are responses they are making but not consciously, like nodding when you are listening to someone you are agreeing with, or smiling slightly. This is called passive responses and once you see these, they are in a trance state.

12. Exercises for Rapport

Now that you know the basics of conversational hypnosis, you can begin to put them all together with these rapport building exercises.

Rapport is the foundation for conversational hypnotism so it is vital that you can build rapport quickly and with great success. Now, you can practice and hone all of the skills you have learned, polishing your abilities with conversational hypnosis.

Exercise 1

Some people are naturals at establishing rapport and others have to work at it more but anyone can learn how to establish rapport. It is a skill and just like any other skill, it can be learned and perfected and for conversational hypnosis, you have to have your rapport skills perfected.

For this exercise, you are going to hone your rapport skills. This requires you to go out and just start talking to people and work on building rapport with strangers. If you are having trouble, use the following guideline and then include some of the tools from the book as well.

- Keep in mind that a smile opens many doors. When people see someone they do not know approaching them to speak, they will be more receptive to an open and friendly smile than if you do not smile. When we see a smile, it helps ease their mind that the encounter might be negative. We are wary of strangers by nature but someone with a genuine smile is going to receive a better response.

- Eye contact is important but do not hold it for too long. You have to be pleasant and polite, smiling and make eye contact. Eye contact is important because if someone will not make eye contact with you, it makes you think they are hiding something. If you make eye contact, it makes you more open and trustworthy.

- Use yes statements to encourage them to agree to you about something, establishing common ground. You can build up a conversation from there.

You should approach individuals, couples, and small groups of people. What you talk about is up to you, but you need to get your feet wet with working with different numbers of people and establishing rapport. Use the above steps to help establish it combined with the rapport tools I have given you.

Exercise Two

For you to be genuine with your audience, you have to really feel positive. If you are trying to build a connection to someone but you are not genuinely positive or happy, they will notice. This is an exercise for you to be able to instantly give yourself a genuine feeling of positive warmth and happiness.

Once you are feeling that way, you can connect to people better because they will just feel that you are being genuine. Out of all of the exercises, this is the one many people have trouble with but it is vital to having success with your conversational hypnosis because without it, you will have trouble being genuine.

Think back to a time when you were genuinely happy. It should be a memory that included a time where you felt warm, happy, and positive. What was going on at the time and how did you feel? You need to focus on that memory and how you felt. The goal is to recreate that very same feeling of happiness.

For this to work, you cannot just examine the memory as if you were looking at a photograph. You have to mentally put yourself into the memory. Relive the moment in your mind, adding as many details as you can remember. You will notice that you are beginning to actually recapture that feeling, just let the feeling grow and develop within yourself.

With more practice, you will be able to recapture this feeling in a manner of minutes, so before you go to meet people or talk to people, take the time to recapture this feeling of warm positivity so you can be genuine when you are talking to people.

Exercise Three

This is an exercise about matching and mirroring. You need to become accustomed to doing this subtly and so it looks natural and fluid.

Go somewhere where you are likely to find large groups of people and just use your peripheral vision to watch how the group interacts. You can find groups or just two people, but you will quickly be able to tell when mirroring and matching is being used because people tend to do this when they are comfortable around someone, without realizing it.

Pay attention to their body language and make sure to notice when someone mirrors and matches the other person. You can learn a lot just by observing. Once you are ready to practice this, you can actually begin using it with people you encounter throughout your day. See if people respond to you differently once you begin mirroring and matching them.

13. What is Hypnotic Language?

If you are expecting a section with special language that hypnotists use, you will be disappointed. Hypnotists, although they do use language in a special way to receive results, do not use any unusual language.

In fact, the more ordinary and everyday their words are, the better their subjects will respond. Hypnosis is a highly evolved skill and there is no magical formula that makes people listen or fall into a trance so how then are hypnotists able to use language and receive results just by talking?

If you have ever been to a hypnotist show, all the hypnotist usually does is talk to the subject; there is perhaps some contact, when putting them deep into trance, but, for all extents and purposes, all the hypnotist does is talk.

Hypnotic language is nothing special; it is just every day, common language. What is special about it is how it is used and spoken and that is where the power of conversational hypnosis comes in.

Hypnotic language, if you ever sit and listen to it, can be repetitive but it is far from magical. It is all about knowing how to speak, what to speak, and the way you say it. That is where the power of conversational hypnosis truly comes from.

Hypnosis works because the brain is able to easily comprehend what you are hearing; the more complex the message, the harder the brain will have to work to decode it and you lose your chance to be influential.

If you heard someone skilled in conversational hypnosis talking, you would not even be able to guess that they were using any conversational hypnosis techniques on you. The reason you would not be able to tell is that the language sounds natural and flows smoothly.

In regular hypnosis, there is a lot of repetition, the same phrases said over and over, and it is often somewhat monotonous to the idle ear. If you put a charismatic speaker and someone who is well versed in conversational hypnosis side by side to talk, you would not be able to pick out who is simply charismatic and who has the skills for conversational hypnosis.

The reason conversational hypnosis is effective is because it uses various linguistic methods to make communication better. Charismatic speakers can do this naturally but these are traits that are learned and modeled after in conversational hypnosis because they make communication powerful.

In conversational hypnosis, you are really just turning yourself into a better speaker, with the ability to clearly and effectively speak to anyone and have them respond positively.

The basic tools that you already know help you to pull in your audience and establish rapport. Without rapport, you cannot ever build that connection of trust that is necessary for you to be able to influence people.

Rapport is built partially through communication and is paired with non-verbal techniques such as mirroring and matching, which you should be able to easily and subtly do by now.

Every word you use with conversational hypnosis is chosen carefully as well as how you are going to say it. Your intention is to receive results when speaking to others and that could be getting them to buy what you are selling, see your point of view, and agree to help or simply to help get a point across.

No matter what situation you are in, you will be able to have a ready arsenal of linguistic tools on hand to use to help you and that is how this book will help. You will polish up the skills you have while learning a more in depth approach to the use of hypnotic language and how it will help you achieve your goals.

14. Hypnotic Language Basics

The next several chapters are all about hypnotic language and how to use it but before going into the specifics about hypnotic language, you need to know a few basics first.

This chapter includes some basic tips and strategies that will make learning the next few chapters easy and effective. Keep in mind, the things that you will learn in this book are the basics of language patterns and linguistic techniques.

Everyone finds a language flow or pattern that works best for them and so instead of learning what is in this book and using it as a script, you need to use it as a foundation for you to adapt and evolve for your own use.

With the basics, you can learn how hypnotic language works and then you can take what you have learned here and make it your own, tailoring it to suit your own personal style.

Imagine if everyone who used conversational hypnosis all said the exact same thing. It would be obvious that they were using linguistic tricks to influence, would it not? But, everyone who uses it changes and adapts it for their own use, taking the basics and the language principles included in the following chapters and then once they are mastered, changes them to suit their needs.

This chapter includes the tips you will need to have the best success learning the basics. Ways to maximize your learning potential so that you not only learn the basics but can also easily mold and adopt your own speaking style into them.

Mentally Rehearse

With language patterns, your ability to put words in a specific sequence is very important. When speaking, you can have a better impact by selecting where and how you put words together. If you switch the order of words, the message may remain the same, but the statement will lack the power of persuasion.

This means that as you are learning, you will need to mentally rehearse what you are going to say before you say it. Once you have learned this, you will be able to flawlessly use hypnotic language patterns with ease, but when learning it, take the time to rehearse what you are going to say in your mind first.

Getting the word sequence right is more important than how quickly you learn to speak and how you keep the conversation flowing. Once you have learned these patterns, you will be able to easily keep conversations flowing, to your benefit!

Write It Down

Writing something down is a good way to help your brain remember it. Reading it is one thing, but the physical act of writing down something that you want to learn and remember actually helps you do so. Keep a notebook handy when you are reading this and when you learn something new, write it down. Keeping notes helps to cement the instructions in your mind for later use.

When you see samples in this book, write them down and then take some time, once you have finished the chapter, to come up with samples of your own. This is an excellent exercise to help you learn and understand what you have read. After all, unless you fully understand the concepts of hypnotic language, you will never be able to successfully use the material in this book.

Create your own samples, making several for each new thing you have learned. Read your samples and compare them to the sample, so that you can tell if they are in line with the material you have just learned. This will be a struggle at first, because you will be learning new language patterns and your instinct will be to write the samples based on language patterns you already use rather than the newer ones you are learning, which will make you a better and more influential speaker.

Sound It Out

In addition to writing it out and practicing writing your own hypnotic language samples on paper, you need to sound it out by practicing out loud. Unless you also practice saying these language patterns daily, you will find that when it comes time to actually put them to use, you are tripping over your own tongue.

It is a lot of work to learn language patterns but not only does this book give you the information that you need to succeed, but it is also telling you how to succeed with it. If you read the book but ignore this chapter, your success will be limited. You need to practice, out loud, every single day, until you can easily speak naturally while using these patterns.

Practice, Practice, Practice

Start off practicing with someone else who has an interest or knowledge with conversational hypnosis. Finding someone who is already an expert to listen to you is an excellent way to get coaching. However, if you do not know anyone, then do not worry, just find a friend you can practice on.

Start using your learned language patterns with your everyday interactions. This will help prepare you for becoming accustomed to speaking naturally and without reading from samples. Remember the first tip, to mentally rehearse so do not worry if you sound awkward or stilted in your speech at first because the more you practice, the more natural you will sound.

Make it a habit to read your samples daily, write out new samples daily, practice saying them out loud, and then making a point to have a few discussions daily with someone, where you use hypnotic language during the conversation.

15. Hypnotic Language Principles

Before going into detail about the various hypnotic language patterns, you need to know some of the principles behind them, the core reasons that hypnotic language allows people to use conversational hypnosis so well.

When learned and used properly, conversational hypnosis allows you to always keep conversations positive, polite, and in your favor. To those listening, you will come off as a very charismatic and skilled speaker and they will never know that you are even using hypnotic language along with conversational hypnosis to help increase the effectiveness of your communication.

That ease of use comes with practice and with a good understanding of how it all works. Many books tell you how to use conversational hypnosis without going into why it works. It is my belief that you cannot understand the how of something without knowing the why of it. Before going into how language is used and how to best achieve success with them, this section will be a brief overview of why they work.

These are the basics that you will be using in every conversation; you will be able to create seamless and effortless communication with others, which will be persuasive and charismatic. This is the art of conversation and below is your building blocks.

Agreement

One of the basics of conversational hypnosis is that you need to be in agreement with the person you are talking to. This means that if they have a different viewpoint as you do, instead of directly challenging them, you find common ground for them to agree on and you work from there.

When you frame your words in such a way that you are not only establishing but also maintaining agreement with the person you are talking to, it makes it easier for them to get into that yes mindset you need. This does not mean that you have to force them to say yes, you can get them to agree to smaller things, while still allowing them to keep their own viewpoint.

This is the exact opposite of the hard sell approach, which puts so many people off because it puts pressure on the subject; this is low key and very subtle. The idea is that you want them to ultimately agree but without feeling pressured.

Plausibility

Plausibility is a fine line that you need to walk; when you are first talking to someone, they are going to have their guard up and so the minute you say anything that does not sound plausible, they will stop listening and you lose your chance to influence them. Plausibility matters, especially in the beginning because they are analyzing everything you say, trying to determine how sincere you are and how much of what you are saying is plausible or how much is just to hook them in.

Everything you say does have to be true. Conversational hypnotism is not about lying to get your way; it is about communicating effectively so that people will want to do it your way. The minute you stretch the truth too much, their mental filters will snap down into place, breaking rapport and making your job of influencing them nearly impossible.

Seamless

As you are talking, you need to be able to easily handle anything the other person says to you quickly. You need to be able to think on your feet with conversational hypnosis because the longer you pause and think about how to respond, the weaker that connection you have built up between the two of you becomes. You need to be able to fluidly link what you are saying and your responses to steer the conversation the way you want it to go.

This requires you to use a variety of techniques to keep them interested and to keep them connected to you. Allowing them to lose interest is a mistake many learners make. You will make this mistake early on but it is necessary when you are learning because it takes time to be able to have a seamless conversation and that skill only comes with practice. That is why the prior chapter is important; it stressed that you need to practice, both in writing and by speaking to others, so you learn how to speak seamlessly.

Connection

Your ability to not only grab the other person's interest but to also hold it and forge a connection with them are vital skills. Without this connection, getting people to listen to you is nearly impossible. If you are not charismatic, personable, and able to use language to draw people in, then you will have a hard time influencing people.

This book assumes that you already have the ability to build rapport. Rapport building is a cornerstone of conversational hypnosis. Using language to help forge and hold a connection along with your already learned rapport building skills will allow you to keep a connection with the person you are talking to.

You can build a connection with language just as you can with mirroring and matching rapport techniques. You can use linking words that help to build ideas and help the person you are talking connect to you and to your message.

Having them respond well to you is one thing but having them respond positively to both you and what you are saying is the goal. This requires some linguistic skills to help you connect your message to the person you are speaking to, drawing them in.

Some of the simple ways to help people connect to what you are saying is by spelling it out for them in plain and simple language and to help link your message to something familiar to them. If you can connect what you are saying to something that is familiar to them, then you are helping them to connect to your message.

Here are the words you can use to help connect ideas:

- Which means
- Because
- And
- As

These are all ways that you can use to link ideas together and this logical linkage of ideas helps the person you are talking to feel that what you are saying has merit and is valid. The more they feel connected to what you are saying and feel they understand what you are saying, the easier it will be to get them to agree to it.

As stated in an earlier chapter, hypnotic language is plain language. It is how you use it that has all the power. These words are small, common, but very powerful because they are words that the subconscious mind will pick up on instantly.

When you use these words, whatever you said prior and whatever you say after this connection word or phrase will be connected in their mind. As you can see, there are a lot of different connections with conversational hypnosis and they are all important.

16. Hypnotic Language Principles – Part 2

This next set of principles all have to do with hypnotic language and how to make it effective. This continuation of the prior chapter has to do with some of the basics you need to keep in your mind when reading the rest of the book.

These are not fast and hard rules but the basics that will help you be able to apply the specific hypnotic language techniques better when you are using them. These are situational principles, which are to be used when in a situation that calls for them.

These principles are here for you to read, understand, and then incorporate into your conversational hypnosis skills. You will not need to use every principle in every situation and sometimes, you might need to use them all. Keep these in mind as you read the rest of the book, because you can easily adapt these with any and all of the techniques in this book.

Repetition

A great deal of hypnosis is repetition. With stage hypnosis or hypnotherapy, it is more noticeable and more of a focus of the trance induction, but those are different types of hypnosis. Even though conversational hypnosis is subtle, you will still use repetition as a hypnotic language tool to help increase the power of what you are saying.

Instead of repeating whole phrases, which can sound forced and unnatural, you will end up repeating only key words, or words you want their subconscious to key upon.

Also, repeating your connecting words of which means, because, and, and as are also ways to hammer your point home. Because the words are so common, you can repeat these connection words and phrases to link two ideas. The other person will be focused on the sentence before and after and less so on the connection words.

Coached Responses

Getting the other person to respond how you want them to respond is another principle of hypnotic language. Naturally, you want them to respond in a certain way but without them feeling forced or compelled to have had to respond to you in a certain way.

Hypnotic language is designed to help you coach the people you are talking to for the appropriate response without them knowing they are being coached.

No one likes to have a hard sell pushed down their throats and if you try it, it will only alienate the people you are talking to and that is the opposite of what you want to do.

You will learn several ways to coach them to want to give a positive response, all of which are subtle, no pressure, and without any force on your part. You will never need to use the hard sell approach ever again with conversational hypnosis.

Rhythm and Tone

Instead of putting someone into a deep trance state, with conversational hypnosis you are putting people into a light trance state, one that allows them to drop their mental defenses so their subconscious mind is more open to what you are saying. One of the ways you achieve this trance state is by your voice.

Your speaking rhythm and your tone are very important factors. If you have a hesitant voice, which is so low that people have to strain to hear you, you will find that no matter how well versed you are in conversational hypnosis, you will have trouble. Using an authoritarian tone will allow people to respond to you better.

When you sound like you have authority, it automatically creates a feeling of trust. People trust people who sound like they have authority and know, without a doubt, what they are talking about. A deep voice that is strong rather than weak is how you sound like you have authority. All too often, people think that the louder they talk, the more authority they will have. This is not the case.

You do not need to blast out eardrums, you only need a voice that carries well and can be easily heard by others. If this means you have to practice talking in a stronger voice, do so; it will help increase the effectiveness of this book.

Your speaking rhythm is also important because the cadence of your voice will help create that light trance state you need the other person to enter into. Cadence and rhythm come with practice. The more you practice speaking with a rhythm, the easier it will be for you, and soon, it will become second nature.

Agreement

You will learn how to frame things so that the other person will be agreeing with you. Once you get someone to agree with you, it is easy to help build up their trust by continuing to get them to agree with something you are saying. Agreement is a powerful tool and you will learn how to use it in various ways.

Agreement helps to defuse any possible resistance you might have from the people you are talking to because, let's face it, when you are talking to someone for the first time, they are all automatically already on guard and ready to resist anything you suggest.

You get them to agree to something small and it helps break the ice, so to speak, about what you have to say. Keeping agreement with your subject is just one of the principles you have to keep in mind.

17. Hypnotic Language – The Agreement Pattern

When trying to influence and persuade, you are naturally trying to get your audience, or the person you are speaking to, to tell you yes. You are looking for a positive response rather than a negative one, which is the dreaded "no". People are naturally skeptical of strangers and even more so of anyone they feel is about to give them a pitch for a service, product, or even just an idea.

The agreement pattern is your way of deflecting the negative responses and the "no" answers you receive in a subtle way. Once someone tells you no and you leave it at that, they have won. They were resistant to what you had to say and you are choosing to let them resist.

No salesman finds success by simply admitting defeat when told no and neither will you. Some try to argue, attempting to break down that "no" and turn it into a yes. However, badgering someone is never a good way to get them to respond to you favorably.

When you use the agreement pattern, you can effectively get someone to agree with you on one point, because you are not arguing with them, you are actually agreeing with something they said, and then adding something of your own for them to agree with.

This is a way to deflect their resistance to you because once you get them to see that you are being agreeable and that you are putting out suggestions they also agree with, they will want to continue to talk with you. This language patterns allows you to continue to get them to agree with something that you are saying every time, keeping the conversation flowing without any arguments.

The basic agreement pattern is simple – I agree with your point (point A) and also this (point B) with point B being the point that you are adding, which will be something they will agree to or find relevant.

For example, if you are selling computer software and the person you are talking to has just told you they feel that the product you are selling costs too much, which is, in this case, point A.

You would use the agreement pattern to reply with this, "I agree this software is more expensive than similar software already on the market and let me add that our software has several built in features that comparable software makers do not have or that you would have to buy separately."

You agreed with them on point A, which it was expensive but you then used "and", a connection word, to add your point B, something that the other person will have to agree with because you should have already gone over the features.

You can either take something they have just said, or something they had previously said to use as point A, the statement you are agreeing to and then add your own point for them to agree with. In this fashion, you are able to build up a dialogue that is flowing freely instead of being one-sided.

If there is nothing they said that you particularly agree with, you can always use a generic, "I do see your point," or "I see what you are saying." Non-committal statements like that allow you to acknowledge they have spoken, without forcing you agree to something you may not agree with.

Lying, when you agree just to use the agreement pattern, is not recommended because if you say something later on that contradicts what you agreed to earlier, it will make them realize that you have lied and they will no longer trust you.

Why does this work? It works because the minute you disagree with someone, they will not only become defensive, but they will also often take an offensive stance as well, challenging everything you say to them.

Disagreeing, no matter how politely, is a subconscious trigger for people to go on guard and prepare for a fight. When you agree with them, even to something small, then they never go on the defensive and because of that, they never go on the offensive with you. The conversation stays amicable and you are able to keep using the agreement pattern to get them to stay connected with you.

The more you use it, the more relaxed with you they will be because they will feel that you are trusted and easy to talk to. Even though you might have a difference of opinion, you are agreeable and humans respond positively to that.

They might tell you "No" but instead of simply rebutting their "no", you are respecting their right to say no and agreeing with something they have said, while making a valid point of your own. This type of back and forth should be fluid and positive.

When you use the agreement pattern, it can help to defuse arguments and stop a heated debate in its tracks. People expect you to jump into the verbal fray and when you use the agreement pattern, you disrupt the argument by interjecting an agreement and then including a statement they can and will agree with. It can turn a conversation around instantly.

One thing you have to be wary of using is the word "but". When people hear that word, they know a disagreement is coming up, you agree with what they said but you are going to follow up with your own disagreement.

You will notice in the sample that we gave earlier, the phrase "and let me add" was used instead of the word "but". This prevents them from becoming defensive, and if you use the word "but" to make your point B, they will become defensive.

You need to learn how to reframe your own rebuttals to avoid using "but" as a way to get your point B across. Once you use the word "but", the person you are talking to will feel attacked; it doesn't matter if you tell them that the sky is blue, they will not want to agree with you simply because they feel that you are in the mood to argue. You always want to avoid creating any sort of feeling that you wish to argue with them in any way.

The agreement pattern means you keep all aspects of your conversation positive. You use no words that will trigger anyone's defenses. Using "and" is better because it helps to link their point, which you just agreed to, and your own point, which will be something they will agree with. Get out of the habit as using "but" in your discussions.

When you use "but", it sounds like you are about to give an excuse. Excuses, although thinly disguised as facts, never leave a good taste in anyone's mouth. Going back to the example, this is how it would sound if you had used the word "but" instead of "and".

"I agree that this software is more expensive than similar software already on the market but our software has several built in features that comparable software makers do not have or that you would have to buy separately."

The second half of your statement now sounds like an excuse as to why your software costs so much instead of a positively framed response about why the extra cost is actually a good value. You want to be able to keep them amicable, keep them interested, and above all, keep them agreeing with you!

18. Using the Agreement Pattern

Now that you understand more about what the agreement pattern is and how to use it to your advantage to help make the people you are talking to feel less resistant to listening to you, you can begin to begin using it.

The more versed you become with using simple agreement patterns, the more you can begin to use more complicated patterns, stacking several phrases that have agreements in them, and then ending with the one thing that you want them to ultimately agree with.

Have you ever been talking to someone and found yourself nodding yes along to the points they were making, even though they were not asking you questions that required a direct response? If so, that was someone using a stacked agreement pattern on you.

Here is an example of using a stacked agreement pattern:

"I agree that this software is more expensive than similar software on the market. I also agree that much of the software on the market today is not user friendly or user intuitive and that as a business owner, you need to have software that is user friendly. I also agree with your statement that most software lacks the features you need unless you upgrade to a better version and that is why our software is such a good value; it includes all of the features businesses need, without requiring businesses to have to upgrade, all of the features are already there. Your statement that, to do effective business, you need to own multiple software programs and that is not efficient for you, as a business owner is also something I agree with. I believe this software will boost your business's productivity and efficiency because it eliminates your need to use multiple software programs."

As you can see, you continue to use agree statements, followed up with "and" statements, and you build and you build until you get to the last statement, why your software is a good choice for them and because you built up such a positive and effective argument, without ever disagreeing with them, they will agree with you. By the time you get to the last sentence, the person will be nodding along with you and that is exactly what you want to happen.

Before you begin using the stacked agreement patterns, you need to become accustomed to using the basic ones first. Here are some basic agreement patterns, using software as the product.

"I agree that this software is on the expensive side and that means you are actually getting several products all included with this one software package, so in the end, this is more cost effective than using multiple programs."

"I agree that all of the features offered in this software can appear to be confusing and let me tell you that they are actually user friendly and there is 24/7 free help desk to any of our clients as well as tutorials and training videos built into our software."

"I completely agree that working efficiently is how companies prosper and that is why our software is designed to streamline the business process so your employees spend less time on repetitive work and more time focusing on the things that matter."

Because conversational hypnosis is used for far more than just salespeople, here are some non-sales examples for using the agreement pattern:

"I agree that I promised to clean the garage and did not and I will go do that and the back patio now."

"I do agree with you that our shared fence needs to be repaired and I will get some estimates for a repair and will pay for half of the cost of repairs."

"I agree that I am not always good at expressing my feelings and I also want to tell you that you are the love of my life."

As you can see, you can really apply the agreement pattern to almost any discussion where you want to be in agreement instead of arguing. You can use this with your partner, your neighbors, your family, your co-workers, and in the course of your employment.

Do not try to use the agreement pattern on people until you are comfortable with phrasing it correctly, which means you need to take time and practice creating your own agreement patterns. Write down your own, making sure you have the phrasing correct and even practice making arguments from the other point of view and then using the agreement pattern to reply.

In addition to writing them down, become accustomed to saying them aloud so you can say the phrases smoothly instead of haltingly. Once you are ready, start using short agreement pattern statements with people and you will see the difference in response.

The more you use it, the less awkward you will be with using them. To be effective, it has to sound natural and that can only be achieved with practice so do not be put out if you feel as if you are not sounding natural at first; you will, just keep at it.

19. Using Agreement Sets

With conversational hypnosis, there is no single language pattern or technique used; there are multiple patterns and techniques that are layered and stacked upon each other. Each language pattern has, at its core, the basic pattern and that pattern can be built upon to form more complex patterns, all with the same core pattern at the heart.

This is how you can use conversational hypnosis anywhere and with anyone because you will be able to know what pattern or what technique will work best at any given time and be able to use it.

Knowing when and how to use the patterns is largely intuitive because there is no set guide for when to use it but rather, it is an intuitive knowledge that will come to you with practice. As you become accustomed to using them, you can easily tell when one pattern is not effective and when another one is.

Agreement sets are a more complex form of the agreement pattern. In the agreement pattern, the main goal was to get the other person to agree with you, on anything.

The idea behind it is that once someone begins to agree with you, they lose their inherent resistance toward what you are saying and thus, influencing them becomes easier. Agreement sets are basically the same, only the end goal is to get them to be influenced. In other words, you are working toward getting them to say yes to something specific.

When you use agreement sets, you are leading the conversation in a specific direction, with the intent to get the other person to ultimately comply with whatever you want them to do.

This could be selling them a product or service, agreeing to help you with something, or used to resolve conflicts at home or at work; it does not matter what the end goal is, only that by the time you are done with the agreement set, the other person will be in agreement with you.

Like the agreement pattern, it helps to break down someone's natural defense to want to say no and remain guarded when speaking to people. Agreement sets help take the guesswork away from getting someone to say yes to you because instead of simply asking and then banking on a simple possibility of getting yes, you are leading them down the verbal pathway to saying yes.

The brilliance of it is that they will not even be aware of the fact that they are being led because it is subtle and not forceful at all.

Like off conversational hypnosis language patterns, the minute you try to force it or to force compliance, you lose the connection you have built up with that person. Your hard work will be for nothing as the other person will feel like they are being pressured and they will disconnect with you and say no.

When you come across someone you do not know, and they begin to pitch something to you, your first instinct is to resist and say no, but you might agree to listen to be polite. You have already decided to say no. However, instead of just a hard sell, the salesperson comes at you with a set of facts, all of which have merit, so you agree.

The more you begin to agree with what they are saying, the more you feel that you can trust them and your instinct to say no to their pitch fades and eventually, you buy the product, without feeling any pressure whatsoever at any time from the salesman. You might even be surprised when you buy it because you know that you meant to say no but the pitch was so compelling.

Here is an example of using an agreement set with someone – In this example, the person speaking is at a business conference, selling business software to people who have just left the demonstration and lecture about the software.

"What a great turn out for this conference, it looks like you have just left our product demonstration and let me tell you that our business software package will streamline how effectively your business runs."

This simple statement actually has three parts to it. The first part is "what a great turn out for this conference", which is a statement that the person the salesperson is speaking to can easily verify and agree with. The second part, "it looks like you have just left our product demonstration", is also something that the person the salesman is talking to can easily verify, as they have just left the area where the speech and demonstration had taken place.

The last part of the statement is not something that the person can personally verify, but because they have just agreed to the first two parts of the overall statement, they will tend to agree because their brain is now in agreement mode with the salesperson. They were right about two out of the three statements, to which the brain logically concludes that they are right about the last part, too, which is "our business software package will streamline how effectively your business runs."

You can see how subtle and effective this is. As long as the leading statements are easily verifiable by the person you are speaking to, you can use agreement sets to ensure compliance and to reduce resistance.

Now, if you had just opened up with the line about how your software will streamline their business, they would wander off because it sounds like a pitch and their defenses go up! But, lead up to that statement and they will suddenly be willing to listen to you, and buy the product.

Now, you can combine the above with agreement patterns to create an even more complex statement that is even more effective:

"Are you enjoying the conference? There certainly is a lot to see here today, is there not. What a great turn out for this conference, it looks like you have just left our product demonstration and let me tell you that our business software package will streamline how effectively your business runs."

As you can see, agreement patterns and agreement sets both work on the same principles and stack well together. You can use them separately or together to increase the effectiveness of what you are saying.

20. Using Thought-Disruption Patterns

No conversation will ever go as smoothly as you want it to go. At some point, you will find someone who has disengaged from what you are saying and you can see that they have done so.

If they start looking around, glance at their watch, or begin to fidget, you are in danger of losing them and you need to do something to get the conversation back on stable ground. Once someone fully disconnects from what you are saying, recapturing their interest is hard.

The thought-disruption pattern is what you use when they are beginning to lose interest and you want to get the conversation back on track. You can also use the thought-disruption pattern if the conversation goes off track or if you find yourself on the defensive and you want to put the other person back into an agreeable state of mind. It is a simple trick but like all of the hypnotic language patterns, it is very effective.

You can use the thought-disrupt pattern to first get the other person's attention, then you can put them back into an agreeable state of mind by using the agreement pattern and then you can use agreement sets to steer the conversation back toward your topic. The subject will be back on track and you will not have lost the opportunity.

It works because they have mentally drifted away from what you are saying so you say something totally unrelated to the topic, either a question or a statement.

They will respond because it will be for a totally new topic and then once they respond, you can set them back to the "yes" state of mind by using the agreement pattern and then you can re-introduce your original topic, and use agreement sets to lead them back to where you want them to be in the conversation.

Timing is important with this because if you wait too long to use the thought-disruption pattern, then you will lose the chance to really put the conversation back on track.

If you use it too early, you might end up breaking the connection you have with the person you are talking to by asking the unrelated question as a way to divert their attention back to you. If they are still paying attention to you and you ask a question that is off-topic, it can leave them confused.

You need to wait until you sense that they are no longer following you closely. If you see them showing signs of disinterest, such as no longer nodding their head in agreement with you, no longer giving you their full attention by looking around or checking their phone or watch, these are the signs that you should use the thought-disrupt pattern to get things back on track.

If they take a few steps away from you, as if to walk away, that is another sign that you need to use the thought-disrupt pattern to get them back on track.

For example, you are at a fair, and you are selling healthy cooking products. Someone is standing there, they had been talking to you, and they had all the signs of being interested, such as nodding along with you, hooked by your intro, and engaging in a discussion, when you notice they are suddenly fidgeting around a lot.

You know by the fact that they are looking around at the people walking by instead of talking to you, that they are about to walk away so you use the thought-disruption pattern by making an un-related statement that will get them to respond.

You can say, "Have you seen the cinnamon rolls at the booth across from the pavilion?"

They will either answer yes or no, but the important thing is that they have responded to you and you have their attention again. Now you can use the agreement pattern to get them to agree with something, such as, "One of the best things about fairs is you can splurge on the food."

Nearly everyone will agree with this and when you see them agree with you, use an agreement set to hook them back into the conversation, "Fair food is tasty, everyone always has their yearly favorites that they go to and then the next day, they start thinking about healthy cooking. Wouldn't you like to be able to cook healthier at home but without a lot of prep? With most cookware, you need to use oil and that just adds fat and calories; wouldn't you love a way to cook without oil but without sacrificing taste?"

They will be back on track. Asking about the cinnamon rolls was the diversion, then you used the statement about splurging on food being one of the best things about fairs to get them into an agreement pattern and then you used an agreement set to lead them back on topic, which is the cookware you are selling.

You can use this anywhere when you need to be able to take control of the conversation again. If someone has taken over the conversation, this works too.

You can effectively use the thought-disruption pattern to get them off the tangent they are on and back onto your topic. You can gently diffuse arguments by using this tactic as well. It can be used in nearly every situation, not just when they start to lose interest, although that is the main purpose of this.

This is simple and effective; all you need to do is disrupt their train of thought by asking a question or a statement they were not expecting. This will startle them slightly, breaking up their own train of thought and shifting their focus back onto you.

21. Using Conversational Hypnosis to Give Criticism

Conversational hypnosis is not just a tool for selling things, although, if that is your profession, it will certainly boost your sales. Conversational hypnosis is about better communication in every aspect, for conversations that are both pleasant and unpleasant. The techniques in this book can be used when talking to your spouse, your family and friends, co-workers, bosses, and clients.

Conversations go smoother with conversational hypnosis because you recognize the importance of that connection that needs to be between you and the other person, the rapport, and you know how to express yourself in a clear and positive way. This is of great use when you find that you need to give negative feedback or criticism to someone but you do not want to anger them or alienate them either.

Not everyone can take constructive criticism and in fact, many people who ask for opinions find that they are ill equipped to actually respect and listen to negative feedback. No one likes being told they are doing something wrong or that it could be better but sometimes, you find yourself in the position where that is exactly what you must tell them.

Bosses walk a fine line with this because it is their job to oversee their employees and offer this type of feedback and constructive criticism and they have to do so because if they see mistakes and do not correct it, the responsibility will ultimately fall on their heads. If they come down too hard on employees or are too harsh, morale drops.

The answer for bosses or for anyone who needs to give feedback that the other person will not want to hear is that they can use conversational hypnosis. The only tried and true way of approaching criticism is that if you give someone positive feedback first and then follow it up with the negative feedback, it makes it okay.

For example:

"I loved your report for the monthly sales and the charts looked great but it had a lot of spelling errors."

"I love the rice you made but the chicken is too overdone."

"That color is the perfect shade for your hair but that new hair cut makes you look several years older than you really are."

"I agree that you have been keeping your room cleaner but you are still piling your laundry up in front of the laundry room."

All of the above statements start off with something complimentary and then after the word "but", the hammer falls. When you hear the criticism at the end of the statement, you no longer care that you were complimented right before that because the negative is what your brain focuses on and so the positive that had come before it is erased from your mind. The word "but" tells them right away that something unpleasant is coming and the entire positive part of the statement is gone. They will focus only on what follows "but".

The problem is that we are so conditioned toward using the word "but" in our conversations. We use it when we are about to give an excuse. For example, "I am sorry I was late but my clock got unplugged." We use it when we want to tag on anything negative, such as in the above examples.

The question becomes, how do you still give the criticism you need, without making the other person feel angry and resentful toward you? Once again, hypnotic language patterns come into play because we have already seen how the word "but" will shift someone's full attention away from the first part of the statement and focus only on what comes after you use the word "but".

You can use this to your advantage because if we, as humans, are conditioned to place our focus and our attention on what comes after the word "but", then why not put the negative things first and then follow up with the good things after the word "but". You simply reverse the order and give the criticism first and then you give the compliments.

So our examples now become:

"Your monthly report had a lot of spelling errors but the information itself was nicely prepared and I loved the charts you made."

"The chicken was overdone but I love this rice you made."

"Your new hair cut makes you look several years old than you really are but I love that color, it is the perfect shade for you."

"You are still piling up your laundry in front of the laundry room but you have been keeping your room clean and I appreciate that."

Can you see the difference it makes? Traditionally, people gave a compliment first so it would soften the blow of what was to come after. It does not soften the blow, it fully erases the fact that they ever been complimented because their mind is focused on the last thing they heard, which was negative. The whole theory of softening the blow does not work.

What does work is knowing that the person you are speaking to will focus on the last part of the statement because when we speak, the things that are important are the things that are at the end of the statement or the question. You are still giving them the criticism and feedback you need to give them but you are doing so in such a way that they hear the feedback and then are immediately given positive feedback, which will be their focus now.

You can now easily hand out criticism without looking like a villain. This works wonders when giving feedback to your kids, your partner, co-workers, and friends. It is amazing how that just by switching the order of the positive and negative parts of a statement, you can change the impact that this has in such a major way.

Will they still be mildly upset at receiving negative feedback? Most likely, but they will remember that you choose to end with a compliment and that will make them feel good.

22. The Importance of Confidence

Confidence is important because if you lack confidence in yourself, no one will want to place their confidence in you. Often, and especially when trying to learn and master something new, that inner voice will speak up, telling you that you are not doing it right.

If you listen to this voice, you end up with a lack of confidence. If you ignore the voice and do your best, regardless of any self-doubts you have, you face the world with confidence.

There are many reasons people lack confidence when it comes to conversational hypnosis, and the biggest reason is that someone is shy and this fills them with self-doubts about being able to approach and talk to anyone with the authority and easy going manner you need to have when using conversational hypnosis.

Confidence is a matter of perception but it is not how other people see you, it is all about how you see yourself.

Your own perceptions of your abilities are what makes you lack confidence and holds you back. If you can shift that perception to a more confident one, then you shed those unhealthy perceptions of yourself in favor for healthier perceptions of yourself and what you can do. In other words, when you let that little voice fill you with self-doubt, it is because that is how you perceive yourself! Change how you perceive yourself and that little voice will have nothing to speak up about and will fall silent.

Confidence is not something you can gain overnight but if you lack confidence and it is holding you back from achieving success with your conversational hypnosis, you need to do something about it. Thankfully, anyone can gain confidence. It is fairly easy and it can be done through the use of this confidence building exercise.

Many exercises have you focus on imagining yourself as a confident and successful speaker but this exercise is a little different. The reason you are not confident when you speak is because you know that you have made mistakes when speaking and because of that, you are always nervous about making the same errors again.

This turns into a vicious circle of nerves and self-doubt. In this exercise, we will help you seek out your errors and then eradicate them from being repeated in the future.

The first step is that you need to find a quiet spot. Choose a place where you will not be disturbed by outside distractions. Make sure you quiet your cell phone, turn off the radio or the TV, and if you are wearing anything even the slightest bit uncomfortable, take it off or change so you are comfortable.

Sit or lay down where you can be fully comfortable, such as a couch, bed, or a chair. Once again, it has to be a comfortable place because if part of your brain is busy thinking about how much your shoes pinch your feet or how hard and uncomfortable the chair you are sitting in is, this will not work.

Clear your mind by taking a few deep breaths and then think back to a recent time when you were having a conversation or speaking to a group and it did not go well. It does not have to be when anything major went wrong, just that you failed to influence or really get a response from the person or the group.

Pick a recent conversation that was not a good one even, such as a stressful discussion with your boss or your partner, or a group meeting where you tried to use conversational hypnosis and failed to get your point across effectively.

Pull up that moment in your head, so you can replay it in your mind, like a movie. See how the conversation started and how it progressed, from start to finish. If you cannot remember the specific words you or the other person said, at least remember how the general tone was and the gist of the words.

How did they respond to you and what had you just said to them to get that response? Take your time and let the memory of the conversation build up in your head so you can remember it as clearly as you can.

Now, going through the conversation, step by step, what went wrong to make it so that you were not able to influence or persuade the other person or the group? Pinpoint all of the areas where you could have altered your responses to receive a better response. Now, go through and mentally list all of the ways you should have responded to get a better response.

Perhaps you used the wrong language technique or you used the wrong words and it triggered a negative response instead of a positive one. How could you have done better? How would you re-do that conversation if you were able?

Now, replay that scenario from the beginning in your mind but instead of using the responses you actually used, use the corrected responses instead and then have the other person respond how you think they would have responded, had you said the correct statement instead of the original. The mistakes you made before no longer matter because you can avoid them now.

Replay the scenario again, seeing yourself being able to give the new responses and get the response you want. See how easy it is and how confident you are when you use the new responses and now you can discard how you felt during that original scenario.

You should do this every night and every time you have had a conversation that failed to go your way. This will help you learn how to correct your mistakes while building up your confidence at the same time. Hold that new attitude and confidence level from the replacement scenario in your head because that is how you will be soon.

After doing this exercise repeatedly, soon you will find that you are running out of material to use because you are making less and less mistakes and that your confidence level is soaring.

23. NLP Representational Systems

You can tell how someone is feeling and thinking by non-verbal cues that are more intimate than simply their basic one language. Humans can lie. There is no way to dance around that fact but because our brains all work the same way; even though someone can try to hide the truth, they have responses that show this and you can use this.

This is not talking about a "tell" like a poker player might use, or a cop would use to tell if something is lying, such as licking their lips or fidgeting with something on their clothing. This is about how we process and access information in our brains and the physical motions we make when doing so.

Naturally, it is to your advantage to be able to tell how someone is thinking when you are talking to them because you can adjust your dialogue accordingly. Representational systems are a part of NLP, or neuro linguistic programming techniques.

NLP uses a feedback-centric approach to resolving problems, including communication and many of the techniques used with conversational hypnosis are related to, or come from, NLP practices and principles.

With NLP, it is important to be able to receive feedback from the person you are talking to.

Naturally, you cannot stop every few seconds and ask for feedback so you need to learn how to get it on your own and that is where representational systems come in. When we process information or access our memories, our eye movement corresponds with a certain representation system.

The different representational systems are how we can tell how something is either recalling or processing something and the eyes are how we can tell. They call it eye accessing cues and by watching someone's eyes, you can tell what representational system that person is using.

There are six in total:

AER – Auditory External Remembered – When this is the system being used, the person is recalling or thinking of something they have heard.

AEC – Auditory External Constructed – This means the person is thinking of something that they are imagining.

AI – Auditory Internal - This is what someone uses when they are thinking to themselves, such as trying to figure out something.

VC – Visual Constructed – This is when someone is creating an image in their mind of something that they construct themselves, it is not necessarily something they have seen in real life.

VR – Visual Remember – This is when someone is recalling things they have seen personally and have the information stored as memories.

K – Kinaesthetic – This has to do when someone is recalling sensations of touch.

Auditory representational systems all have to do with things that are heard, such as real and recalled imaginary and constructed in the brain and our inner dialogue to ourselves. Real and recalled sounds are our memories of actual sounds, constructed sounds are those that we are making up because we have not heard them, and then there is our inner dialogue, which is a sound only we can hear.

Visual representations systems are the same, based on what we can remember seeing and things we imagine. For example, you may not have seen a giraffe in person, but you have seen picture or seen them on TV so you can recall what a giraffe looks like. However, if someone asks you to think of a talking ice cream cone, that is something you need to create in your mind.

The kinaesthetic representational system is what is triggered when someone is feeling the sensation of being touched or recalling the memory of how a certain sensation felt at a time when they were touched.

How can this be useful? If someone is telling you they have seen a purple giraffe but their eye access cues tell you that they are making up the image instead of actually recalling it, you will know that they are lying and bluffing. This gives you an edge. You can tell by their eye cues if they are speaking from memory or lying and making something up.

Another way this is useful is that you can tell which system someone accesses more often. Are they accessing sounds more, the feeling of touch more or visual more? Some people prefer sight over sound and some people can remember how something sounds over how it looks. When you can tell how they are accessing their information, you can begin using that to your advantage.

When talking to someone who accesses their visual centers more, use visuals when talking to them to lead them down the path you want them to go. For someone who accesses their auditory centers more, use sound as a way to pace and lead them to where you want them to go in the conversation and if they prefer touch, then invoke the sensation of touch in how you talk to them.

Here are the eye cues you need to look for:

Looking up – When someone looks up, they are accessing their visual representational system. If they up and to the right, that is their visual constructed system and upper left is visual remembered, an actual memory.

Looking sideways – When someone looks to the left or to the right, they are accessing their auditory representational system at that time. If they look to their right that means it is the auditory constructed system and if they look to the left, that is auditory remembered, something they have actually seen.

When someone is accessing the kinaesthetic representational system, they will look down and to the right.

If someone looks down and to their left, they are accessing their inner dialogue and are actively thinking about something. When you see them doing this, you know you have them thinking very seriously about what you are saying.

You can subtly use this information. For auditory people, use the word heard and other words that have to do with sound. For visual people, use the word see and other words that have to do with sight and seeing. It will help build and keep rapport and make it easier to influence.

24. Putting It All Together

Now, you have all of the information, you just need to put it all together and then keep working at it until conversational hypnosis comes to you as easy as regular conversation used to. You will have stumbles and setbacks but that is to be expected.

Conversational hypnosis involves using a whole new way of communication and that takes time to learn. If anyone tells you that you can learn it instantly, you can file that under "too good to be true".

The only real skills you can possess are the ones that you learn and this book has the skills you need to turn your basic knowledge of conversational hypnosis into a skilled, advanced user of conversational hypnosis. However, there are still some tips you need that will help you put all of this together, ensuring that you have success.

First, you need to express what you want to say through both verbal and non-verbal cues and that means you need to experience it before you express it. For example, if you are leaning over the counter and you tell someone, without much enthusiasm, "Hey, you will love this new cookware system," they will probably just pass you up. If you cannot muster up enthusiasm, why should they?

You have to put yourself into the state of experience so when you move and when you speak, you convey, through every fiber of your being, the emotion that you are expressing.

In the same example, if you were standing up tall and looking alert and someone walked by and you leaned toward them, smiling and with your eyes bright, and said, "You will love this new cookware system" while you gestured toward the display, they will see you are enthusiastic and hear that you are enthusiastic and will stop to listen.

The next thing you need to do is keep in mind how you emphasize certain words. When you emphasize a word slightly with your vocal tone, that person's subconscious will pick up on it and they will pay extra attention to that word. Using your tone of voice is important because you can really show how passionate you are or convey emotion and importance.

Your tone needs to match the message you are giving. If you are talking about something serious, an upbeat tone is not appropriate. Likewise, if you are talking about something upbeat and use a serious, somber tone, you will find you have trouble getting the person you are talking to connect with you.

Emphasis on certain words also makes the other person pay attention. You can say something like, "The pancakes here are amazing." But if you keep your tone the same throughout, the person you are talking to might just think that you are using the word amazing, but that the pancakes are probably not that amazing. However, if you say, "The pancakes here are amazing!" and you emphasize the word amazing, you will get your point across that the pancakes are to die for.

You can alter the meaning of the sentence slightly, depending on what words you add extra inflection onto. Write out a few standard sentences, such as, "I love this movie" and "Why did you say that?" and then practice saying it, only changing the inflection you put on different words.

For example, you can convey a lot of emotion by changing your inflection. Take the word "right" and then decide how to say it so that it signifies agreement, a question, disagreement, and a statement. Depending on how you say the word, you can make it mean any of the above.

25. Conclusion

Conversational hypnosis is all about communication skills. We communicate all the time but so often, we are not good at it. With conversational hypnosis, you will learn how to be a better and more effective communicator, someone people will naturally want to listen to and to follow their advice. Being an influential speaker is important for many reasons and these are skills that can be learned.

This book will help you become a great speaker, just as effective as the people who seem to be natural, charismatic speakers. Communication is all about the connection; if you can connect to your audience, then you can communicate with them better. However, we are not taught how to connect to people, just how to talk. Talking is not the same as communicating and now that you have read this book, you know how to communicate.

When you talk to people, you have to establish rapport because that connection helps them feel as if you are trustworthy.

Rapport is the center of conversational hypnosis, because you cannot influence someone without having a strong rapport with them. Your responses to your audience are also important because it helps to strengthen that connection with them.

Keep in mind that your conversation should be engaging, and you need to grab and hold your audience's attention, using the conversation hooks that were covered in the book. When someone is comfortable asking you questions, the conversation will flow naturally between you, helping to establish trust. Mirroring and matching helps you to establish rapport, just be careful to not go overboard with it.

Your detective skills will help you tell how well they are responding to you; pay attention to body language, tone, and to what your audience is saying. The previous chapter includes exercises for rapport building so that you can help sharpen your skills.

The best thing about conversational hypnosis is that you have ample chances to try it out every day. Think about how many people you interact with every day. Every single one of those people is someone you can practice with. Be friendly, be positive, and start talking!

Language patterns are patterns we all respond to in certain way. Our brains are programmed to respond to certain things in a certain way. If you are trying to communicate something and influence someone, this allows you to break down their natural defenses so you can get them to trust you, relax, and more importantly, listen to you.

Two of the most powerful hypnotic language tools you can use are the agreement pattern and agreement sets. The reason these work is because once you can get someone to begin to agree with you, they will be more apt to continue to do so. It is a language and communication principle that holds true for nearly everyone.

The thought-disruption pattern is the technique you will use when you need to regain someone's attention or to steer a conversation back on track. It works because when you switch to an unrelated topic when the other person is not paying attention, you can quickly get them back into a "yes" set of mind using agreement patterns and agreement sets.

Your confidence level dictates your success, which is why you need to make sure you present yourself as an authority figure and if you have any doubts, get rid of them. You need to know that you can do this and that you will do a great job. Use the confidence building exercise to help increase your confidence if you need help with that area.

Representational systems are how you can tell how someone processes information. Some people focus on what they hear and others on what they see and others on touch. By using words that invoke the representational system they use the most, you can help connect them to your message easier.

The only way to perfect your skills is to practice. Practice your skills wherever you are and with whoever you are talking to. Soon, you will be able to easily influence and persuade smoothly, just like the experts.

Made in the USA
San Bernardino, CA
11 July 2016